Curriculum Visions

Changing Britain

vol 1: 1948–1969

Dr Brian Knapp

1950s school children

Curriculum Visions

There's much more online including videos

You will find multimedia resources covering a wide range of topics at:

www.CurriculumVisions.com

CurriculumVisions is a subscription web site.

A CVP Book
Copyright © Earthscape 2007–2009

First edition 2007. Revised edition 2009.

The right of Brian Knapp to be identified as the author of this work has been asserted by him in accordance with the Copyright, Designs and Patents Act 1988.

Author
Brian Knapp, BSc, PhD

Editors
Jan Smith (former Deputy Head of Wellfield School, Burnley, Lancashire) and Gillian Gatehouse

Senior Designer
Adele Humphries, BA, PGCE

Designed and produced by
EARTHSCAPE

Printed in China by
WKT Company Ltd

**Changing Britain vol 1: 1948 to 1969
Revised edition – Curriculum Visions
A CIP record for this book is available from the British Library**

ISBN 978 1 86214 604 4

Illustrations
Mark Stacey

Picture credits
All photographs are from the Earthscape Picture Library, except the following (c=centre t=top b=bottom l=left r=right): *British Airways page 42; Chiltern Open Air Museum page 1bl, 10; Corbis pages 18, 19; East Saltoun primary school pages 2, 3, 23; Imperial War Museum pages 8–9, 11; Mary Evans pages 35, 44–45; NASA page 40b; ShutterStock pages 1br, 4bl, 18br, 24, 26, 29b, 32–33b, 33, 36tr; TopFoto pages 5, 6, 12–13, 15, 16, 20, 22, 27, 28t, 29t, 32t, 37tl, 38–39t, 41, 43. The publishers have made their best endeavours to contact all copyright holders for material published in this book.*

This product is manufactured from sustainable managed forests. For every tree cut down at least one more is planted.

Contents

Words in **BOLD CAPITALS** are further explained in the glossary on pages 46 and 47.

Note: in this book the term 'Britain' is used as a shorthand, meaning "The United Kingdom of Great Britain and Northern Ireland".

1960s school children

Britain in the 1930s

Britain was a divided country, with great hardship in old factory areas and prosperity in new parts of the Midlands and South. Meanwhile, war loomed ever closer.

This is a book about life in Britain from after World War II until the end of the 1960s. To understand that time, you need to know a little of what Britain was like before the war.

A nation divided

If you had lived in 1939 and looked back on the previous ten years, what you might have said about life in Britain would have depended where you lived. If you lived in the North, it probably would have been a mean, hard time, with many around you out of work. If you had lived in the South, you might have become wealthier, you could afford to buy your own car and even buy the new electrical goods on sale in the shops.

People describe this time as "A nation divided". How did it come to be like this?

The North

It all started during Victorian times when Britain was made very wealthy by factories and workers who lived by our great coal fields. These were

◀ ① The original 1930s Monopoly counters were made of cardboard and wood.

1930s timeline

The average national wage was £175 a year for a minimum 48-hour week.

Sticky tape and the jet engine invented. Pluto discovered.

Sliced bread available.

First TV broadcasts begin.

Air conditioning invented.

Scientists split the atom.

Cat's-eyes invented to show the centre of a road at night.

Parker Brothers sells the game 'Monopoly' (picture ①).

It is now possible to bring meat from the **COLONIES** using new refrigerated holds in ships.

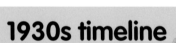

1930	1931	1932	1933	1934

Nylon invented.

Adolf Hitler becomes Chancellor of Germany.

Loch Ness monster first spotted.

in the Midland Valley of Scotland (centred on Glasgow), in the North East of England (centred on Newcastle), on the Pennine areas (centred on Manchester and Leeds) and in South Wales centred on the mining valleys. At this time Britain was called "the workshop of the world" because other countries could not compete with us.

But in the 20th century things started to change. Much of the wealth of Britain was drained from the country by World War I. In 1929 most of the world's businesses collapsed. Britain made much of its money by selling things abroad. Now fewer people abroad could afford to buy our goods, so factory owners and coal mine owners had to sack their workers. It was a desperate time, but it affected the Victorian boom areas based on textiles, iron and steel, coal mining and shipbuilding most (picture ②).

Conditions only got better in the late 1930s when we needed ships and planes for the approaching war. At this time factories became busy again.

▶ ② In 1936, shipbuilders of North East England marched from the Tyneside town of Jarrow to London to protest they had no food to feed their children. In these areas millions of unemployed and their families queued at soup kitchens.

There are enough cars on British roads to make the government start the driving test for motorists.

The BBC begins the first regular TV broadcast, but it reaches only a handful of people in London.

Penguin books are founded to give good quality, affordable novels. Before this time such books were very expensive.

Air mail post to anywhere in the British Empire started.

Billy Butlin opens the first holiday camp.

World War II begins.

(For details on World War II please see the 'Children in the Second World War' book.)

1935	1936	1937	1938	1939

Jarrow march for jobs.
King Edward VIII abdicates.
King George VI becomes king.

Prime Minister Chamberlain announces 'Peace in Our Time'.
Ballpoint pen invented.
Gas masks are given out to all British civilians.

The South

At the same time many new inventions were appearing. People setting up new factories for these new industries, based on motor cars and making electrical goods such as wireless (radios) and washing machines, chose the Midlands and the South of England. So many towns in the southern half of the country grew rapidly.

This was a time when large areas of semi-detached houses were built (picture ③). Houses were advertised as being built in the fresh air and away from factory smoke. People could now live in these places because they could use the new buses to get to work.

▲ ③ A row of semi-detached houses in the 1930s. The style is called 'mock-Tudor'. Family cars were still unusual and few homes were built with garages.

Women at home

Most women stayed at home. In those days it really did take all day to look after a home. There were no washing machines in 1930. Clothes were washed and scrubbed by hand, then squeezed through a **MANGLE** and hung out on lines to dry.

Cleaning the house was a matter of sweeping it out with a broom.

As there were no refrigerators, people had to buy fresh food daily. As few people had cars, women had to carry all of their shopping home in shopping bags. No wonder they did not want to trudge very far. As a result, local shops were still the places most people visited.

But there was one way that women could shop that didn't involve heavy carrying. In the 1930s, home shopping was brought to Britain from America. The first was Littlewoods Home Shopping, developed by the same people who had invented the idea of Football Pools in 1923.

The radio and the cinema

By the 1930s fewer people were visiting the **MUSIC HALLS**. Instead they were turning to the radio (called the 'wireless') for their entertainment or going to the cinema. More than 20 million people went to the British cinema each week, making it the most popular form of entertainment (picture ④).

▼▶ ④ **Stars of 1930s cinema: Ginger Rogers on the set of the film 'Swing Time' and (inset) the popular young actress, Shirley Temple, at home with her dolls.**

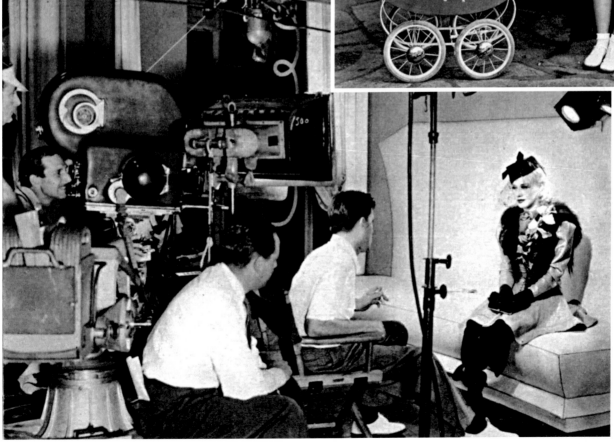

Britain in 1945–1949

Britain was one of the ALLIES who beat Germany and Italy in Europe, but Britain was now an exhausted and impoverished country. It was a battle to survive. Nevertheless, some vital new changes to schools and health were introduced.

World War II lasted six years, from 1939 to 1945. At the end of the war, many countries in Europe were in a poor way – both those who were defeated and those who had won. Britain had spent much of its national wealth buying arms from America. It had turned most of its factories from making goods for people, to making guns, aeroplanes and other war necessities.

The struggle to keep going

The end of the war did not mean everyone lived happily ever after. On the contrary, there had to be an enormous struggle just to keep going, and at the same time to try to rebuild a life for the future.

Baby boomers

Many important events happened just after the war. For example, airmen, sailors and soldiers came back home and were released from the forces – it was called being 'demobbed'. Each person was given a plain suit and a small amount of money. Then they had to find work – something that was not easy.

1945–1949 timeline

First meeting of the United Nations.

Jitterbug dance craze reached Britain from the USA.

London Heathrow airport is opened.

The Second World War ends in Europe.

TV broadcasting starts up again (it was suspended during the war).

1945

1946

◀ ① **1946 was the first year after the war and many children were born. It was called a baby-boom year.**

During the war women had done many of the jobs in factories that men had done before the war. So after the war women felt they could go to work, too. In time this made families with two wage-earners much wealthier, as we shall see.

No let-up in rationing

During the war, Britain had had to try to feed itself as best it could by using as much farmland as possible and also controlling the amount of food people could buy. This was called **RATIONING**.

At the end of the war rationing did not stop. This was because Britain had little money to buy food from overseas. At that time you could put all of the food one person was allowed on ration for a whole week onto one small tray. This is what it was like:

> 1oz cheese; 2oz tea (about 20 teabags worth); 2oz jam; 4oz bacon or ham; 8oz sugar; 1 shilling's worth of meat (a few ounces); and 8oz fats of which only 2oz could be butter.

By 1946 even bread was rationed. Most rationing went on until 1952, and didn't finally end until 1954.

As couples got back together again, so it was natural that many children were born. In time they would be called the years of the **BABY BOOMERS**, meaning that the number of babies being born rose quickly, or boomed (picture ①). All through the next years these baby boomers would find themselves setting new **TRENDS**.

Railways **NATIONALISED**.

National Health Service (NHS) founded, giving free health care for everyone.
The first Morris Minor car is made.
SS Empire Windrush docks at Tilbury with the first in a wave of migration from the Caribbean to England.

George Orwell wrote a book simply called '1984'. It foretold the gradual growth of the government until it controlled everything. In it is the term 'Big Brother' meaning that the state is watching over you all the time.

1947   **1948**   **1949**

The great rebuilding

As the war ended, people looked around our cities and saw great open spaces where bombing had destroyed houses and factories. Many temporary houses (called prefabs – prefabricated bungalows) were placed on these bomb-sites so that people had somewhere to live temporarily (pictures ② and ③).

▼▶ ② These pictures show the recreated post-war prefab at the Chiltern Open Air Museum.

▲ The outside.

▲ The living room with gas fire, mantle clock, the three flying ducks, embroidery over chair back, wooden-cased wireless (the word radio was not used at this time) and books for entertainment (no TV).

◀ The kitchen with mangle and boiler (only a few homes had washing machines). Most items were made of metal or wood as plastics were not common.

▲ ③ **Prefab being assembled.**

These prefabs had gone up quickly, so people began to think that they could continue to build this way, making houses in factories and then simply bolting them together on site. As you will see, this had an enormous effect on people in the 1960s and 70s.

Education

During the war, the government tried to find some time to think ahead. They knew they needed a better school system.

In 1944 the government passed a law dividing secondary schools into three different types: grammar schools; secondary technical schools; and secondary modern schools.

To work out which pupils should attend which school, pupils in their last year at primary school took an exam known as the 11+. However, the number of grammar schools stayed small and few technical schools were built so most people went to secondary modern schools.

You have to remember that before this few **WORKING CLASS** children went to seondary school at all, so although the new system had problems, it was an important step in getting more education to the working classes. School leaving age now became 15 (raised to 16 in 1972). The same Act also ensured all state schools had daily prayers. This was only relaxed in 1988.

The NHS

The government also wanted a better way of treating the sick. Before the war, if you were ill you had to pay the doctor and, if you were poor, you went without treatment altogether.

Lord Beveridge came up with a scheme as early as 1942 for making health care free to all. The Labour government turned this into law in 1948.

No new hospitals were built, the change was that the doctors, dentists, and nurses, were now paid by the government and everyone at work paid for the service through **TAX** according to how much they earned, which is still what happens today.

A new beginning to multicultural Britain

The Empire Windrush was a ship that is an important part of the history of multiracialism in Britain (picture ⑤). The passengers were the first large group of West Indian immigrants to Britain after World War II (picture ④). It was the beginning of modern MULTICULTURAL relations which were to change the face of Britain. In 1998, an area of public open space in Brixton was renamed Windrush Square to commemorate the fiftieth anniversary of the arrival of the West Indians.

The Empire Windrush was an ex-troop ship sailing from Australia to England via Kingston, Jamaica. An advert in a Jamaica newspaper offered cheap transport on the ship for anybody who wanted to come and work in Britain. At that time, there were no immigration restrictions from citizens of one part of the British Empire moving to another part.

The arrivals were first housed in an air-raid shelter near Brixton, South London. Most did not intend to stay in Britain permanently, but in the event most made Britain their home.

▲ ⑤ The SS Empire Windrush.

◀ ④ Immigrants arriving in Britain on the Empire Windrush.

New arrivals

Just before the war, Britain had let a large number of people come into the country from Europe, as they fled from the Nazis. They included Poles and Jews. At the end of the war, many German and Italian prisoners of war chose not to go home.

In fact, because Britain needed to rebuild, it needed as many workers as it could get, and so extra Europeans were welcome.

Then, on 22 June, 1948, nearly 500 people from Jamaica and Trinidad arrived on the SS Empire Windrush. These were the first people from the 'new colonies' who, over the decades, were to have such an important impact on Britain.

Britain in the 1950s

In the 1950s people began to shrug off the effects of war. At the same time, new materials led to new clothes and new products (like TVs) changed the way people lived.

When the 1950s started, food was still rationed and clothes looked much like they had before the war.

Young people did not know about fashion. Fashion was something that people worried about when they were in their 20s and 30s. Fashion was what film stars wore, or people who were very rich.

Most people in the years after the war were not rich, and the money they had only allowed them to buy ordinary clothes.

Children wore school uniforms, a dress for girls, a jacket, cap and short trousers for boys. Girls aged 18 would look just like their mums.

But during the 1950s, the hardships of the war were overcome.

The first important year was 1951 when Britain tried to shake off the war years by staging a Festival of Britain exhibition (picture ①).

This was the time when visitors looked at designs, colours and fabrics that most had never seen before.

1950s timeline

The world population is 2.5 billion. (Now 6.5 billion) British population 50 million (now 60 million).
Only 1 in 7 British families owned a car.
The average British yearly salary is £101.
Average family had 2.2 children, (3.5 children in 1905); now 1.7 children.

The Eagle boys comic magazine goes on sale. The Eagle sells 900,000 copies on its first issue. It features space pilot hero, Dan Dare.

First credit cards issued in USA.

Teddy boys fashion begins.

Polio vaccination invented.

Clean Air Act introduced in 1952 stops all but smokeless fuels. It is designed to get rid of life-threatening winter smogs.

The four minute mile is broken by Britain's Roger Bannister.

'The Lord Of The Rings' published.

First red double decker Routemaster bus on London's roads.

First broadcast of Hancock's Half Hour.

1950   1951   1952   1953   1954

To cheer up the nation, the Festival of Britain was staged in London.

'The Archers' begins on the Home Service radio (now Radio 4). It was meant to help tell farmers about new techniques in an easy to listen to style.

Queen Elizabeth II crowned in June 1953.

Mount Everest conquered by Hillary and Tensing.

One of the first new plastics (polyester, of which many of our clothes are made) is produced.

Ian Fleming writes about James Bond.

▲ ① A drawing showing the Festival of Britain exhibition, 1951. Look for the rocket-shaped skylon. The Festival Hall still remains.

What is more, they were designed for ordinary people. Nevertheless, they were still treated as luxury items. The government wanted to sell as much as possible overseas, so in the early 1950s the British could see the glamour, but they could not buy it in their own shops.

In the early 50s, people had no TV and their rooms were mostly floored by **LINO**. Fitted carpets were unknown.

The felt-tip pen is introduced.

Bill Haley's 'Rock Around the Clock' is the first record to change teenage music.

Bazaar boutique opens in Chelsea by Mary Quant with clothes for young people only.

Sputnik 1 the first satellite to orbit the Earth is launched by the Russians, starting the Space Age.

Premium Bonds started.

First boutique opens on Carnaby Street, London.

Barbie dolls invented.

The microchip is invented. It will soon become the heart of every computer.

First West Indian-style carnival.

1955   **1956**   **1957**   **1958**   **1959**

Britain loses control of the Suez canal in Egypt. The days of world power by Britain are coming to an end.

Velcro fastening invented.

London Transport sends a recruiting team to Barbados.

First supermarket opens, copying USA style of shopping.

First appearance of the 'classic' black taxi cabs.

The first stereo LP records are made.

Notting Hill race riots.

Blue Peter begins on BBC Children's Television.

15

◀ ② Televisions for sale in 1955.

The importance of TV

In 1953 Queen Elizabeth II was crowned. Millions crowded around their neighbour's tiny television set. For many it was the first time they had seen a television. Just after this, sales of televisions boomed (picture ②) and people all over the country could see fashions and trends for the first time.

▼ ③ In the 1950s boys wore short trousers to primary school and a jacket and tie in their teens. Girls wore flared skirts after the American fashion. Long-playing and single records replaced the older '78s'. Meccano was a favourite boy's toy. The first new designs reflecting the 'space age' were seen in objects like newspaper racks.

Television, perhaps more than anything else after the war, was to change everyone's lives. It changed the pace of life and it made people more than ever aware of how they looked, what their homes were like, and even about places and events overseas. Television did more for fashion that anything else and allowed trends to be set quickly and changed again just as quickly (picture ③).

More money, more fashion

By the 1950s, people had got fed up with the drab, plain styles of the war years. They were looking for glamour, but people still had little money.

How did young people move away from traditional styles? One cheap and simple way was by changing their hair style.

In the early 1950s pony tails became fashionable. Then, as people began to change styles, and products such as hair lacquer sprays were invented, so the hair style grew and was puffed up and artificial hair pieces added. By the end of the 1950s, there was the beehive style with a huge amount of hair piled up (picture ⑤).

By the middle 50s people earned enough money to be able to have their hair done professionally. By 1955 almost 30,000 hair salons had sprung up in Britain.

This was the time of the tight waist and the long, full skirt, that flared out when you twirled around (picture ④), and the pencil slim tubular skirt.

▼ ④ The fashion for jiving was much more informal than in the past.

▼ ⑤ The beehive.

▼ ⑥ Gramophones were made in large cabinets. Notice also the telephone in the background.

A whole new range of items to go with clothes – we now call them accessories – appeared, including popper beads and wing-shaped spectacles. But women still wore stockings. Shoes had high heels and by the mid 1950s women were wearing stiletto heels so thin they could puncture a soft wooden floor!

Teenagers

During the early 50s, most people who had their hair styled were in their middle 20s or older, but then came the word teenager. Before this time teenage girls were still girls and boys were called youths.

What changed was that teenagers began to go out and earn money.

As a result, companies took their needs seriously.

The year fashions changed for ever was 1956. In this year fashion, for the first time ever, was affected by what teenagers wanted.

This was probably also the time when what we now call 'CONSUMERISM' began. But BRANDING had not at this stage been thought of.

By the mid 1950s teenagers got their own fashions, own music (picture ⑥), own cafés, own milk bars and even their own transport in the form of scooters. Because they were keen to try out new things, teenagers suddenly became the most fashionable people in both clothes and hairstyles.

▼ ⑦ A teddy boy and girl, 1954.

Teddy boys

Most young men still wore a blazer or jacket, and that was thought fashionable at this time.

A few wanted to be different. They looked back to the Edwardian age (early 1900s). The word teddy is a nickname for Edward (picture ⑦).

Teddy boys wore a long knee length jacket with cuffs of velvet. They wore narrow **'DRAINPIPE' TROUSERS**, shoestring ties and suede shoes with **CREPE** soles. A suit like this would have cost a teddy boy something like 5 weeks average wage!

Boys slicked back their hair with **BRILLIANTINE** and had long sideburns. Another common haircut was called a Tony Curtis – copied from the way the film star wore his hair (picture ⑧).

▼ ⑧ Tony Curtis.

▲ ⑨ A 1950s wireless. Only medium, long and short waves were available. There was no FM.

Wireless (radio) in the 50s

In the 1950s, wireless was the main source of entertainment. A wireless then might cost several pounds, and with wages at £4 to £5 a week, they were a big expense.

Wireless were worked by **VALVES**, and as valves were large, so wireless were also large (picture ⑨).

You listened to stations mainly operated by the BBC on long and medium waves. The programmes were called the Home Service (now Radio 4), the Light Programme (now Radio 2) and the Third Programme (now Radio 3).

If you wanted the latest records, however, then the BBC was not the place to go. Instead you listened to Radio Luxembourg (which really did come from Luxembourg because the BBC was the only British broadcaster allowed in the 1950s) on medium wave. Radio Luxembourg had the first DJs and the first adverts.

◀ ⑩ Elvis Presley in 1965. Elvis is widely recognised as starting a new era in music.

Idols

A whole range of new stars and new music came onto the scene during the 1950s.

It started with Bill Haley and 'Rock Around the Clock'. Bill Haley was middle aged, but Elvis Presley was young and handsome (picture ⑩).

Elvis Presley was the first real rock and roll star who rose to stardom in 1954 with the song 'That's all right'. His most famous song, 'Love me tender,' was recorded in 1956.

Boys wanted to copy his looks and style, girls wanted to go out with boys who looked like Elvis.

But not everyone wanted to look the same. So two quite different groups of people formed: greasers and preppies (see the film 'Grease' for the look).

This first took off in the USA and then spread to Britain. Greasers had black leather jackets and denim jeans. They often owned motorbikes. Preppies, by contrast, chose a neat, tidy look. Boys had narrow ties and suede shoes. Girls wore full pleated skirts (with petticoats underneath to hold them out), and scoop neck blouses with a scarf knotted cowboy fashion at the side.

School children in the 50s

What might you have worn to school in the 1950s? You would certainly have worn a school uniform both in primary and in secondary school. Your mum or gran would probably have knitted your school jumper or cardigan (usually grey) and you would have worn sandals or lace-up shoes. Boys would have worn short trousers (picture ⑪) until they were teenagers.

You would have carried your lunch in a satchel. If not, at school you may well have got a free lunch and you would certainly have had a third of a pint of free school milk (metric measures did not come in until 1971).

But things were changing. Some people were already bringing their lunches to school in a brightly coloured mesh bag made of a new range of plastics.

▼ ⑪ The 1952 class at the East Saltoun Primary School, East Lothian, Scotland.

23

Toys and games

It was during the 1950s that plastics became more widely available, but in the early 1950s, you still played with toys made from metal and wood.

Hoops and frisbees

Using a hoop is an ancient past-time. The word 'hula' was added by sailors using a name for dancing from Hawaii as early as the 18th century. It was then reinvented as a plastic toy in 1957 by the American Wham-O toy company. The hula hoop became the most widely sold toy of the 1950s with 100 million sold in two years.

The frisbee was another reinvention. It began when American university students used the metal pie plates from the Frisbee Baking Company to throw about during lunch. This was then modified and made from plastic in 1957. It was like a large plastic dinner plate that flew through the air and could be used by groups of people as a game. It soon reached Britain and is still a popular toy.

Dinky toys and Meccano

Frank Hornby was one of the most important British toy makers and inventer of Hornby trains. To go with the trains he developed miniature accessories, such as cars.

▲ ⑫ An original 1950s Dinky model racing car.

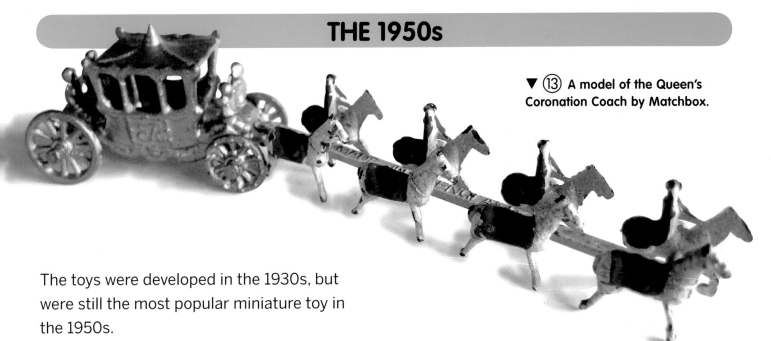

▼ ⑬ A model of the Queen's Coronation Coach by Matchbox.

The toys were developed in the 1930s, but were still the most popular miniature toy in the 1950s.

Dinky toys (like Hornby trains) were typical of early metal toys. Dinky toys were cast in metal and were quite heavy (picture ⑫).

Hornby and Dinky were made by the Meccano Company, who also made metal kits that could be bolted together into anything you wanted (picture ⑭). As people became more prosperous in Britain in the 1950s, so new models of trains and cars were produced.

Meccano was taken over by their rival Triang in the early 1960s, but the age of metal toys was fast drawing to a close.

Another metal toy producer was Matchbox Toys, whose tiny model of the Queen's coronation coach sold over a million in 1953 (picture ⑬).

▼ ⑭ An original 1950s Meccano instruction booklet.

MECCANO

INSTRUCTIONS for OUTFIT No 1

COPYRIGHT BY MECCANO LIMITED
BINNS ROAD, LIVERPOOL 13, ENGLAND   54.1

How we shopped in the 1950s

If you were to go to a high street grocers, such as Sainsbury's, in the 1950s, you would go to a relatively small shop with counters down both sides. The counters would have marble tops and behind them stood assistants waiting to serve you.

You asked for what you wanted, for example, half a pound of butter, and they chopped it off a big block and patted it into shape using wooden **SPATULAS**. They then wrapped it and handed it to you in brown paper. You then paid for it and moved on to the next part of the store where you did this all over again, perhaps buying bacon.

In the 1950s, supermarkets did not exist. Because there was no way of keeping fresh food, it had to be bought each day.

Routemaster bus

In the 1950s, more cars were appearing on the roads and in cities this was causing congestion. Two vehicles were designed during this time which have now become world famous.

The Routemaster was introduced in 1956 (picture ⑮). It had an open platform at the rear which allowed large numbers of people to get on and off quickly at stops or anywhere the passenger fancied, such as at traffic lights if the bus was stopped.

There were many versions of the Routemaster, but the one that is famous across the world was first produced in 1956.

▲ ⑮ A model Routemaster.

◀ ⑯ A model black taxi.

Black cab

The black taxi cab was designed as a vehicle for the busy streets of London and Glasgow and was later used in many other cities (picture ⑯). They could carry five passengers and had a turning circle of just 25 ft which meant they could weave in and out of busy traffic.

Milk was brought to you each day in bottles by a milkman who might still have a horse-drawn cart.

What we ate in the 1950s

In 1952, when Queen Elizabeth came to the throne, Britain had not recovered from the war and sugar, butter, cheese, margarine, cooking fat, bacon, meat and tea were all still **RATIONED**. Even those foods not rationed were often in short supply.

In the 1950s families ate more bread, vegetables and milk than most people do today. Diets were high in fat. A popular snack was dripping (the fat that comes from cooking meat) on bread! You cooked using lard (which was also meat fat). The typical family was still thought of as mum, dad and two children who all ate Sunday lunch with gravy. The adverts "Aaah...Bisto" and the Oxo family were some of the first TV advertisements.

With few refrigerators and almost no freezers there was no frozen food (such as frozen peas or fish fingers) on sale (picture ⑰). People could buy only what was in season. As a result, you could not, for example, get salad in winter. In winter you bought tinned fruit in syrup.

Because people did not earn very much money, food took up about a third of the weekly wage (today it is much less).

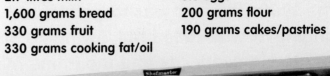

What people, on average, ate each week in the 1950s:

2.7 litres milk	3.5 eggs
1,600 grams bread	200 grams flour
330 grams fruit	190 grams cakes/pastries
330 grams cooking fat/oil	

▲ ⑰ A kitchen unit showing foods from the 1950s.

Britain in the 1960s

In the 1960s the war was forgotten and teenage fashion was constantly changing. It was called the 'Swinging Sixties'. New tower blocks of flats appeared in every city and the Prime Minister Harold Macmillan coined the term, "You've never had it so good".

The 1960s saw many young people change what they looked like and how they behaved. It all began with mods and rockers, and ended with the hippies. It was the decade of the Beatles.

▶ ① The rockers rode motorbikes without crash helmets, dressed in leathers and their idol was Elvis Presley.

1960s timeline

World population 3 billion. 1 in 3 Britain families owns a car. Average UK male annual salary £190.

Doc Martens boot developed. They would be worn by mods, skinheads, punks and goths over the next decades.

Rachel Carson publishes 'Silent Spring', the first book warning of how we are ruining our environment.

Commonwealth Immigrants Act limits the number of people who can come from new colonies.

First James Bond film is 'Dr No', starring Sean Connery. Over half the people in the world have now seen a James Bond film.

The Beatles record in Abbey Road studios.

The store Habitat introduces people to modern design that most people can afford. This begins to change the way people furnish their homes.

'Top of the Pops' TV pop music show begins (and runs to 2006). The first song is The Beatles' 'I Want To Hold Your Hand'

First Notting Hill Carnival held on the August Bank Holiday weekend, a celebration of West Indian culture.

| 1960 | 1961 | 1962 | 1963 | 1964 |

Soviets launch first man in space – Yuri Gagarin.

The Beatles appear at the Cavern.

President JF Kennedy assassinated.

Martin Luther King Junior makes the "I Have a Dream" speech.

'Dr Who' TV series starts, featuring the tardis and the Daleks.

▼ ② **The mods wore designer suits covered by 'army-style' Parka jackets. The more extreme gangs carried coshes and flick-knives. The mods rode Vespa or Lambretta scooters. Their pop idols included The Who.**

Mods and rockers

From the early 1960s some young people – often those from working class backgrounds – began to choose two quite different fashions. They were known as mods and rockers (pictures ① and ②).

Because these people formed in gangs, they sometimes clashed, especially at popular seaside resorts in summer. But this didn't last long because the new hippy culture was on its way.

The Who's first single is released.

'I Can't Get No Satisfaction…' was the first number one for The Rolling Stones.

London's East India Docks are closed. This is because of a revolution in the way goods are moved. Just a few years before, containers were invented. The dockyards of many cities become wasteland until they are rebuilt in the 1980s.

The Beatles release 'Sergeant Pepper's Lonely Hearts Club Band' album.

Monty Python's Flying Circus begins.

Americans land on the Moon. Everyone in Britain says, "That's one small step for man; one giant leap for mankind".

Concorde makes its first supersonic flight. Concorde's speed, combined with the time difference, meant the plane could arrive in London before it had left New York!

1965   1966   1967   1968   1969

The miniskirt arrives.

Star Trek series.

England win the World Cup, including the famous remark "They think it's all over…it is now!" (made by Kenneth Wolstenholme)

Last Routemaster bus built.

First black woman police officer.

Led Zeppelin became famous. They would record 'Stairway To Heaven' which is still the most played song on the radio in the world.

Boutiques

Shops started to open which only sold clothes and accessories for young people. These became known as boutiques. For the first time it was possible to buy a skirt, or a shirt on its own, and mix it with other items. These items became known as separates. Before this time, separates were not common!

As boutiques were opened, the term 'Swinging London' was coined and British fashion influence spread across the world.

Whole areas of London like the King's Road and Carnaby Street were transformed as boutiques took over. Boutiques introduced self-service, unlike traditional clothes shops where you had to be served by an assistant. They also played modern music in-store and gave a new and exciting atmopshere to shops.

The boutiques introduced the miniskirt. It was meant for very slim, even skinny, young women. The most famous model of the time was called Twiggy. The skirt might only be 25 cm deep and was designed to show off young shapely legs. At the same time false eyelashes and pale makeup became fashionable.

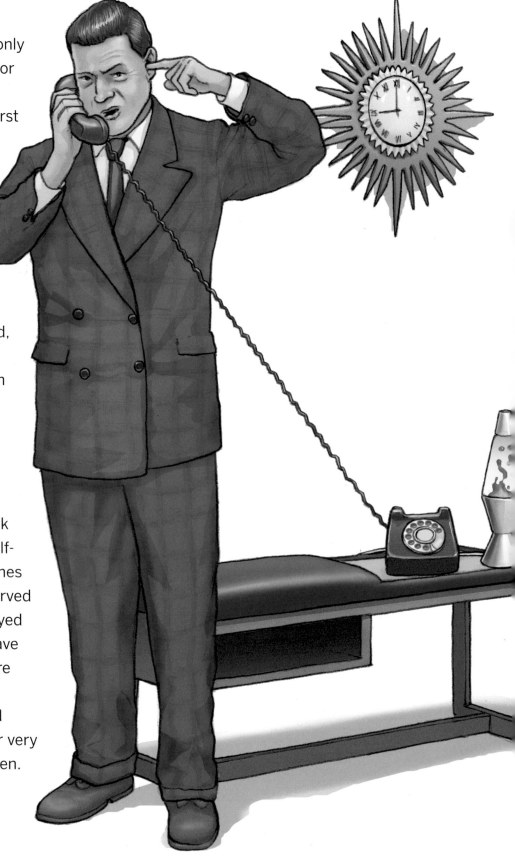

While hair in the 1950s had been in a great beehive that could look too big for the head, in the 1960s it was long and straight (picture ③).

The 60s were also a time of plastics, including shiny, wet-looking PVC. They were fun to look at even if they were hot and sweaty to wear.

▲ ③ The 1960s were a time of great change. People wanted to shake off the formal clothes of the post-war years. Bell-bottomed trousers and miniskirts became fashionable. Furniture was made in a new 'modern' style using new plastic coverings. Older adults kept the style of the 50s so there was a big contrast between the way young and older people looked.

▼ ④ The Beatles in 1964.

Beatles decade

On 9 February 1961, The Beatles first performed at the Cavern Club in Liverpool, but it was not until 1962 that they recorded 'Love Me Do' and became an instant success (picture ④). The Beatles were the best-selling popular musical group of the 20th century. In Britain they released more than 40 different singles, albums and **EPs** that reached number one. In 1965 they received the MBE award for services to their country.

▼ ⑤ A hippie VW camper van. These vans were popular with young people through the 60s and 70s.

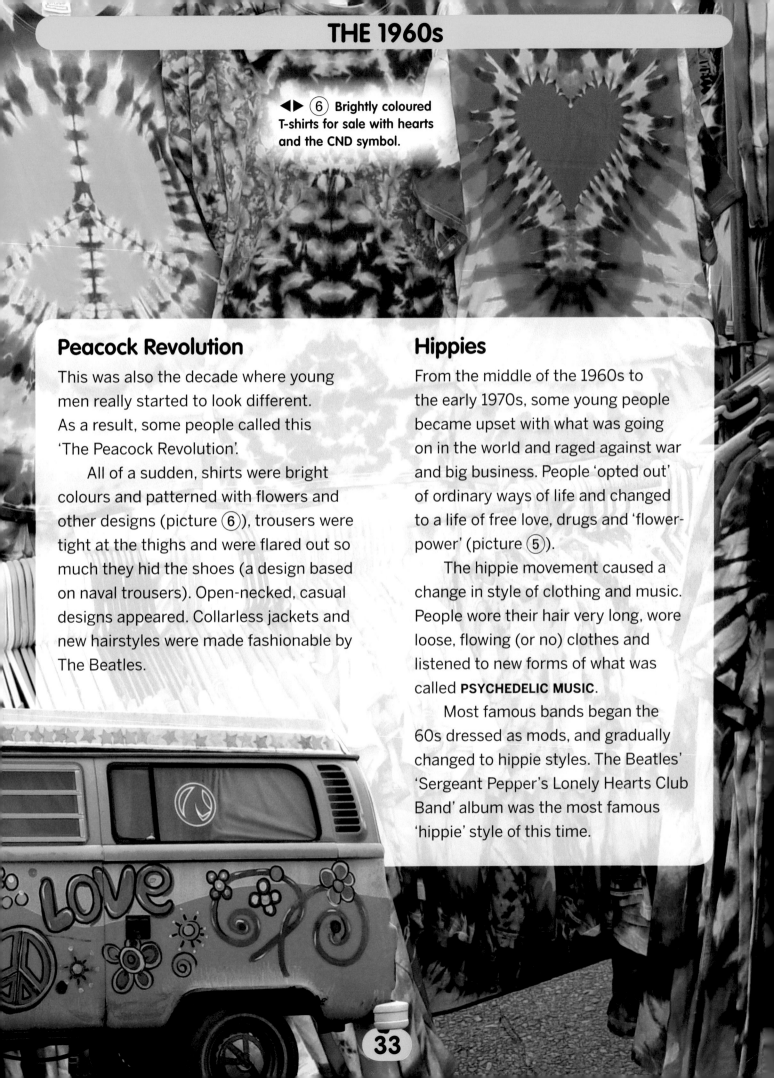

◄► ⑥ Brightly coloured T-shirts for sale with hearts and the CND symbol.

Peacock Revolution

This was also the decade where young men really started to look different. As a result, some people called this 'The Peacock Revolution'.

All of a sudden, shirts were bright colours and patterned with flowers and other designs (picture ⑥), trousers were tight at the thighs and were flared out so much they hid the shoes (a design based on naval trousers). Open-necked, casual designs appeared. Collarless jackets and new hairstyles were made fashionable by The Beatles.

Hippies

From the middle of the 1960s to the early 1970s, some young people became upset with what was going on in the world and raged against war and big business. People 'opted out' of ordinary ways of life and changed to a life of free love, drugs and 'flower-power' (picture ⑤).

The hippie movement caused a change in style of clothing and music. People wore their hair very long, wore loose, flowing (or no) clothes and listened to new forms of what was called **PSYCHEDELIC MUSIC**.

Most famous bands began the 60s dressed as mods, and gradually changed to hippie styles. The Beatles' 'Sergeant Pepper's Lonely Hearts Club Band' album was the most famous 'hippie' style of this time.

Television

Television was still new to most people in the 1960s (picture ⑨). Broadcasting hours were also limited.

In many homes, time was set aside to look at TV as a family event, it was not on continuously as it is now.

In 1967, the first colour television arrived. The BBC introduced a new channel called BBC2, which showed '**GRITTY**' programmes such as the drama 'Z-Cars' (picture ⑦). A new independent television station, paid for by advertising, arrived. It showed 'Danger Man' and 'The Prisoner'. Roger Moore became 'The Saint' and 'Star Trek', made in America, became a hit in Britain, "boldly going where no man has gone before".

◄ ⑦ Z-Cars annual from the 1960s.

Soap operas and more

In 1960, Granada TV launched 'Coronation Street' (picture ⑧). It was the first of the serials shown at dinner time and that came to be called 'soap operas' because the advertising was often about selling soap flakes to housewives.

ITN created the first half-hour evening news bulletin, 'News at Ten', and the BBC created the science series 'Horizon'. 'Match of the Day' was also first broadcast in 1964.

1960s television for children was a time of 'The Magic Roundabout' and 'Thunderbirds', 'Andy Pandy', 'The Woodentops' and 'The Flowerpot Men'. For older children 'Dr Who' and the Daleks began in 1963.

The global village

Television changed the world into a '**GLOBAL VILLAGE**' where everyone could see the same thing at the same time.

People in Britain saw scenes of war between America and Vietnam, they saw **CIVIL RIGHTS** marches in America, and they started to learn about **APARTHEID** in South Africa.

▼ ⑧ A scene from Coronation Street.

Young and successful

TV shows like 'That Was The Week That Was' made fun of politicians and their actions (picture ⑩). 'Private Eye' magazine did the same. They were making the point that the country did not need to be run by a few stuffy wealthy people, but could be run by people like themselves.

Television showed that people with talent could succeed, regardless of their background or schooling. People like Mary Quant showed women could be as successful as men.

▲ ⑩ A TWTWTW (That Was The Week That Was) scrap book created in the 60s from newspaper cuttings about the show.

▼ ⑨ The term record player replaced the word gramophone (see page 19) and record players became 'portable'. Note the television behind.

Weblink: www.CurriculumVisions.com

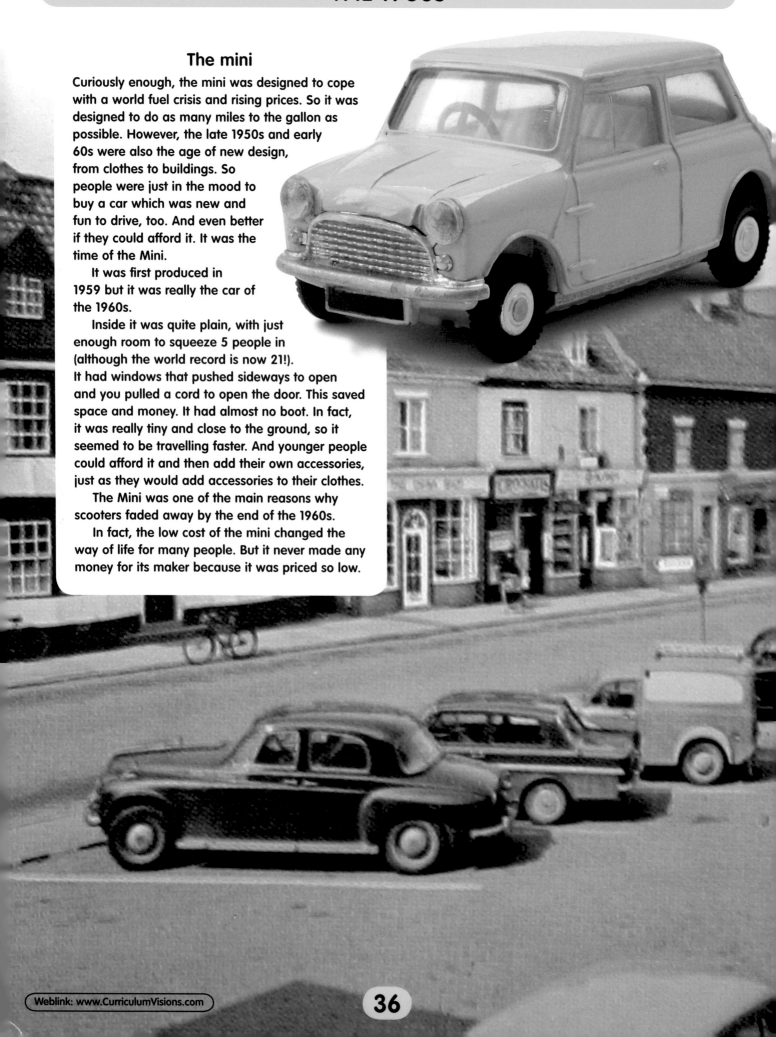

The mini

Curiously enough, the mini was designed to cope with a world fuel crisis and rising prices. So it was designed to do as many miles to the gallon as possible. However, the late 1950s and early 60s were also the age of new design, from clothes to buildings. So people were just in the mood to buy a car which was new and fun to drive, too. And even better if they could afford it. It was the time of the Mini.

It was first produced in 1959 but it was really the car of the 1960s.

Inside it was quite plain, with just enough room to squeeze 5 people in (although the world record is now 21!). It had windows that pushed sideways to open and you pulled a cord to open the door. This saved space and money. It had almost no boot. In fact, it was really tiny and close to the ground, so it seemed to be travelling faster. And younger people could afford it and then add their own accessories, just as they would add accessories to their clothes.

The Mini was one of the main reasons why scooters faded away by the end of the 1960s.

In fact, the low cost of the mini changed the way of life for many people. But it never made any money for its maker because it was priced so low.

The Range Rover

The Range Rover (first called the Road Rover) was another car that began life in the late 1960s and was finally sold to the public in 1970. For many years all terrain vehicles called Land Rovers had been popular with farmers. In 1964 the Range Rover was made to appeal to those with more money and who wanted a luxury Land Rover. Soon, to be seen in a Range Rover was very desirable. Range Rovers became town vehicles for the wealthy. They were to become known as 'Chelsea tractors', because they had the power of a tractor, but you needed to be wealthy enough to live in London's Chelsea to own one.

Many market towns had not seen much modernisation by the 1960s. Chain stores and supermarkets were yet to have an impact. Notice how few cars there are in this picture.

Weblink: www.CurriculumVisions.com

▶ ⑪ Far right, a reproduction 1966 'Colour Change' Barbie doll. Her hair and clothes could change colour when painted with the special applicator.

▲ ⑫ An original 1960s Action Man space suit echoing the space race.

Toys and games

Because television was still new to most people, many toys were made to copy the stars of the shows.

Many girls were attracted to the new fashions coming into the shops for teenagers. The world's most well-known and best-selling doll, was first made in 1959, but it was really a toy of the 1960s. The first Barbie doll wore a black and white 'zebra-striped' swimsuit (page 15) and topknot ponytail. The dolls were available either as blondes or brunettes (picture ⑪). Later, Barbie dolls were produced with other hair

▲ 1960s style children's clothing at playtime.

11+ and comprehensive schools

Until the 60s, most British children had to sit an exam called the 11+ in their last year at primary school. Those who passed went to grammar schools, while those who didn't went to technical or secondary modern schools.

Grammar schools encouraged students to go on to take O-levels and A-levels, whereas most secondary schools taught practical subjects, such as metalwork. In 1964, the Labour Government introduced the comprehensive system in secondary schools, with everyone going to the same type of secondary school. The 11+ was abolished in most schools.

GCEs were taken by some and the easier CSEs (Certificate of Secondary Education) by others (later combined into GCSE).

Lots of new schools were built, but the quality was poor and they are now in need of frequent repairs.

styles and colours. The doll was marketed as a 'Teen-age Fashion Model'. She even had her own boyfried. A British-made fashion doll, Sindy, was produced in 1963.

Action Man was a favourite boy's toy of the mid 1960s (picture ⑫). He was modelled on a soldier and so boys could use him in imaginary war games. He had rubber 'gripping' fingers and eyes that moved.

The 'Space Race'

The race to get the first man to the Moon was between the then Soviet Union (now Russia) and the USA. But the whole world also became excited by space.

Television allowed people to see all of the developments as the Russians kept beating the Americans until the very last moment, when the Americans were the first to land on the Moon (picture ⑭).

Huge amounts of money went into the space race. But this had benefits for everyone because the research gave us new kinds of materials, new medicines and new electronic gadgets.

A space song 'Telstar' went up the pop charts (picture ⑬) and the first words spoken by Neil Armstrong as he stepped onto the Moon, "One small step for man, one giant leap for mankind," became one of the most famous sentences ever spoken.

▶ ⑬ Sheet music for 'Telstar' by The Tornados, complete with photograph of the Telstar satellite.

▼ ⑭ The Apollo mission landing on the Moon in 1969.

▼ ⑮ The London to Aldermaston CND rally, and below, a badge with the CND symbol.

CND

The time from the early 1950s to the middle of the 1990s was known as the Cold War. America and its allies (including Britain) prepared for an attack by the Soviet Union and its allies. They did the same. While no war actually took place, each side stockpiled a huge number of missiles that could fire on their opponent's cities. These missiles were special because they carried nuclear bombs.

CND was formed as the Campaign for Nuclear Disarmament at the start of the 1960s. It was a movement that tried to explain that many people felt the danger of nuclear war was just too ghastly to think about and that all nuclear weapons should be destroyed. This was not to be, but many people made mass protests and, in the 1960s, an annual march from London to Aldermaston in Berkshire (a centre for nuclear arms research) took place (picture ⑮).

CND was an important organisation until the mid 1960s. Its symbol was a circle with three spokes inside.

What we ate in the 60s

People no longer had to ration their food as they had in the early 1950s. They were also earning more money. As a result, British eating habits started to change.

In the 1960s, fish and chips was still the nation's favourite dish. However, the first cooks were seen on TV, led by Fanny Craddock and her husband (in evening dress!). They showed people what they could make with the foods that now crammed supermarket shelves. The range of goods in Sainsbury's, for example, doubled from 2,000 lines to 4,000 lines during the 1960s.

People began to take package holidays overseas (picture ⑯), and so they ate new foods which they wanted to continue eating at home. Spaghetti Bolognese, for example, had never been eaten widely in Britain before the 60s.

▼ ⑯ A British European Airways flight in the 1960s.

▼ ⑰ **Advert for frozen Birds Eye fish fingers.**

What people, on average, ate each week in the 1960s:

2.75 litres milk	4.5 eggs
1,300 grams bread	340 grams cooking fat/oil

At the same time more Asian people arrived, some setting up Chinese and Indian restaurants. They were an immediate success.

People had enough money to buy more meat and they added more sugar to their foods. One way this happened was that cereals were sold already coated with sugar. The amount of sweets sold soared.

Most food that was to be stored, was sold dried or in cans. If you went around a supermarket in the 60s tins still dominated the shelves. The famous slogan 'Beanz Meanz Heinz' dates from this time.

But new ways to make food last longer were being introduced. The steamed, sliced white loaf ('Wonderloaf') became popular because it would last longer than oven-baked bread.

Then air transport became more common and some fresh vegetables and fruit were flown in so that seasonal foods could be on the shelves all year.

Many people bought refrigerators with small freezing compartments. The most advertised food then became frozen foods, with characters such as Captain Birds Eye advertising frozen fish fingers (picture ⑰). These were pre-cooked foods that only needed heating. It was the start of the 'ready meals' era.

The rise of the supermarket

Towards the end of the 1950s there was a shortage of people to work in shops and the government encouraged stores to go self-service, using an idea from America (picture ⑱). Today's Tesco was the first supermarket to start this way. At the same time stores became much bigger, and the term 'superstore' was introduced.

Food was no longer given to you by the assistant, but sold pre-wrapped. As a result, makers competed to make their packaging look most attractive.

Another big change took place in 1964. Before this time, makers set a standard price and that was what was charged in every store in the country. When this rule was abolished, the big shops like Tesco and Sainsbury's were able to sell more cheaply. The food price war had begun.

◀ ⑱ **A 1960s self-service supermarket. Notice the wire basket, which was a new feature of such stores. Before that, people had always taken their own shopping bags to the shop. People had still not got used to a weekly shop and so they bought in relatively small amounts. This mother and her child are wearing miniskirts.**

Glossary

ALLIES The people who were on the same side as (allied to) Britain in the Second World War. They included Australia, Canada, New Zealand, India and the United States.

APARTHEID A system of keeping races apart that existed in South Africa up until 1993. People of different races were not allowed to use the same schools, hospitals, buses or even beaches.

BABY BOOMERS Children born in the late 1940s and who were part of a large increase in the number of children being born. This was because of men coming back home from the war.

BRANDING The way that many companies give a memorable name to their products (just as the book you are reading is branded *Curriculum Visions*).

BRILLIANTINE A kind of oily, perfumed hairdressing that men used to hold their hair in place.

CIVIL RIGHTS The rights of people within a country to personal freedom. In America the Civil Rights Movement wanted to end racial discrimination against African Americans.

CND These letters stand for the Campaign for Nuclear Disarmament. It was formed at the start of the 1960s. The group campaigned for the destruction of nuclear weapons, and made an annual protest march from London to Aldermaston in Berkshire (a centre for nuclear arms research).

COLONY A country that does not govern itself, but belongs to another country.

CONSUMERISM The idea that the main thing people were interested in was buying goods.

CREPE A form of spongy rubber with a crinkly surface.

DRAINPIPE TROUSERS Trousers that were the same narrow width from the ankle to above the knee. This made the trousers look like drainpipes.

EP Short for extended play. These were records that played for two to three times as long as a single.

GLOBAL VILLAGE A term meaning that everyone is now connected so easily using TV, radio, telephone (not computers because they had not been developed at this time) that the whole world could communicate as easily as if they had been visiting neighbours in their local village.

GRITTY A programme with lots of realistic difficult situations that some viewers might find uncomfortable to look at.

LINO A hard, waterproof floor covering that was bought as a strip off a roll. It was made from an early form of plastic. It had a patterned surface and so looked decorative. It was the first time floors had been completely covered. Before that floorboards or stone flags were dotted with mats. Lino was cheap and was replaced by carpet as people became more wealthy in the 1970s.

MANGLE A simple way of wringing water from washed clothes by feeding clothes between two rollers. The rollers were turned by hand.

MULTICULTURAL The idea that a country contains a wide range of people with their own ways of living that they brought with them from the place where they, or their parents, were born.

MUSIC HALL A theatre from Victorian times. People would go to the music hall and be entertained by singers and comedians.

NATIONALISED Becoming part of the property of a country.

PSYCHEDELIC MUSIC Music where the instruments play in a way that tends to flow about rather than follow an easily predictable route.

RATIONED/RATIONING
The government instruction to reduce the amount of food everyone could buy. This was necessary during and after the Second World War because food in particular was in short supply and the government wanted to make sure everyone got at least the minimum needed for a healthy diet.

SPATULA A kind of long-handled spoon, usually with a flat 'paddle' at the end rather than the dished shape a spoon would have.

TAX The money a government collects from wages and the sale of goods and services. It uses this money to pay for hospitals, police, roads and so on.

TREND The style that was in fashion at the time.

VALVE A piece of electronic equipment that was used in wireless (radios) and TVs before transistors and silicon chips were invented.

WORKING CLASS A term that used to be used for people who worked as labourers.

Index